Don't Let The Teddy Bear Fly The Plane

Written & Illustrated
By
H.B. Scribbles

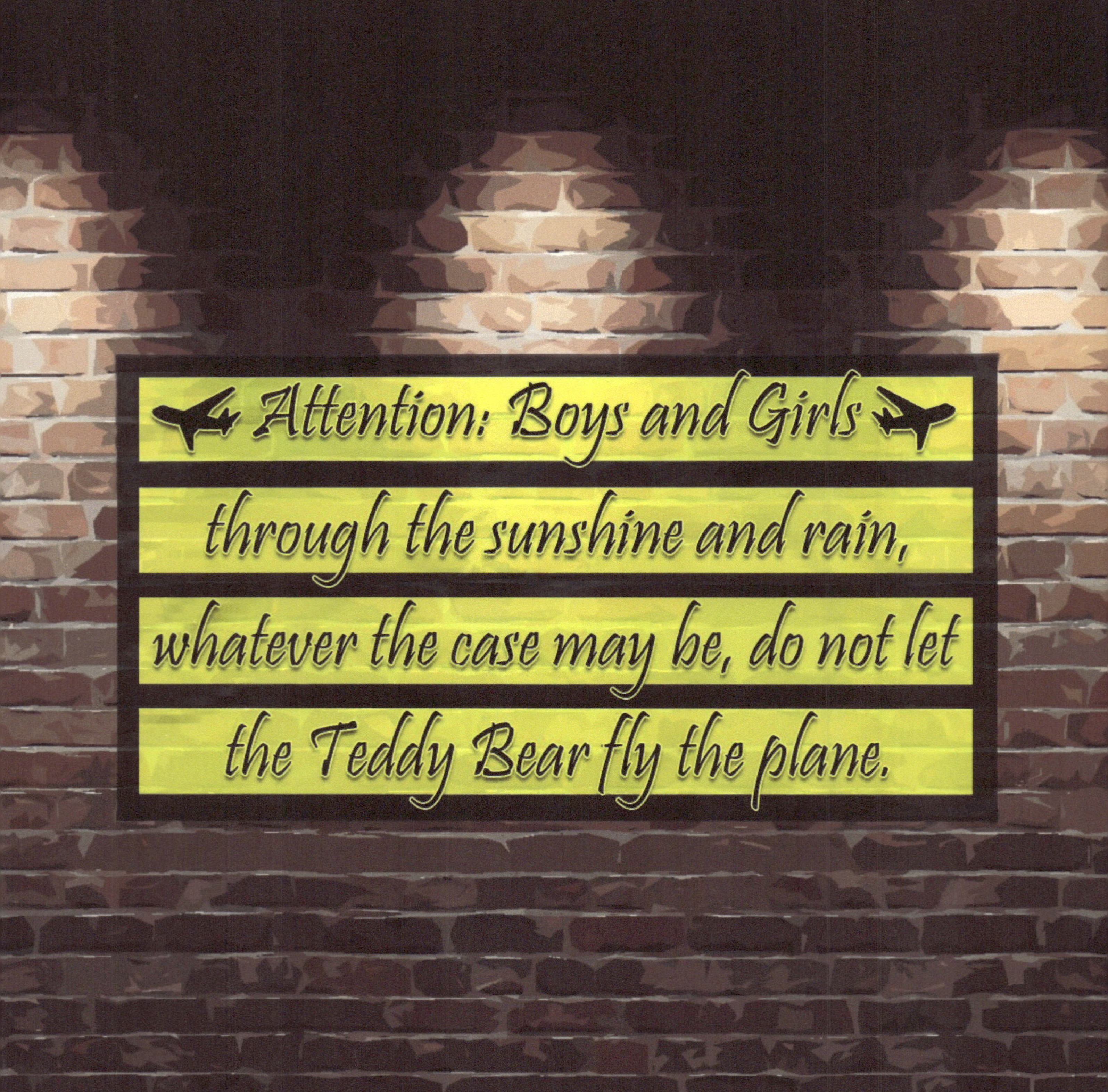

Attention: Boys and Girls
through the sunshine and rain,
whatever the case may be, do not let
the Teddy Bear fly the plane.

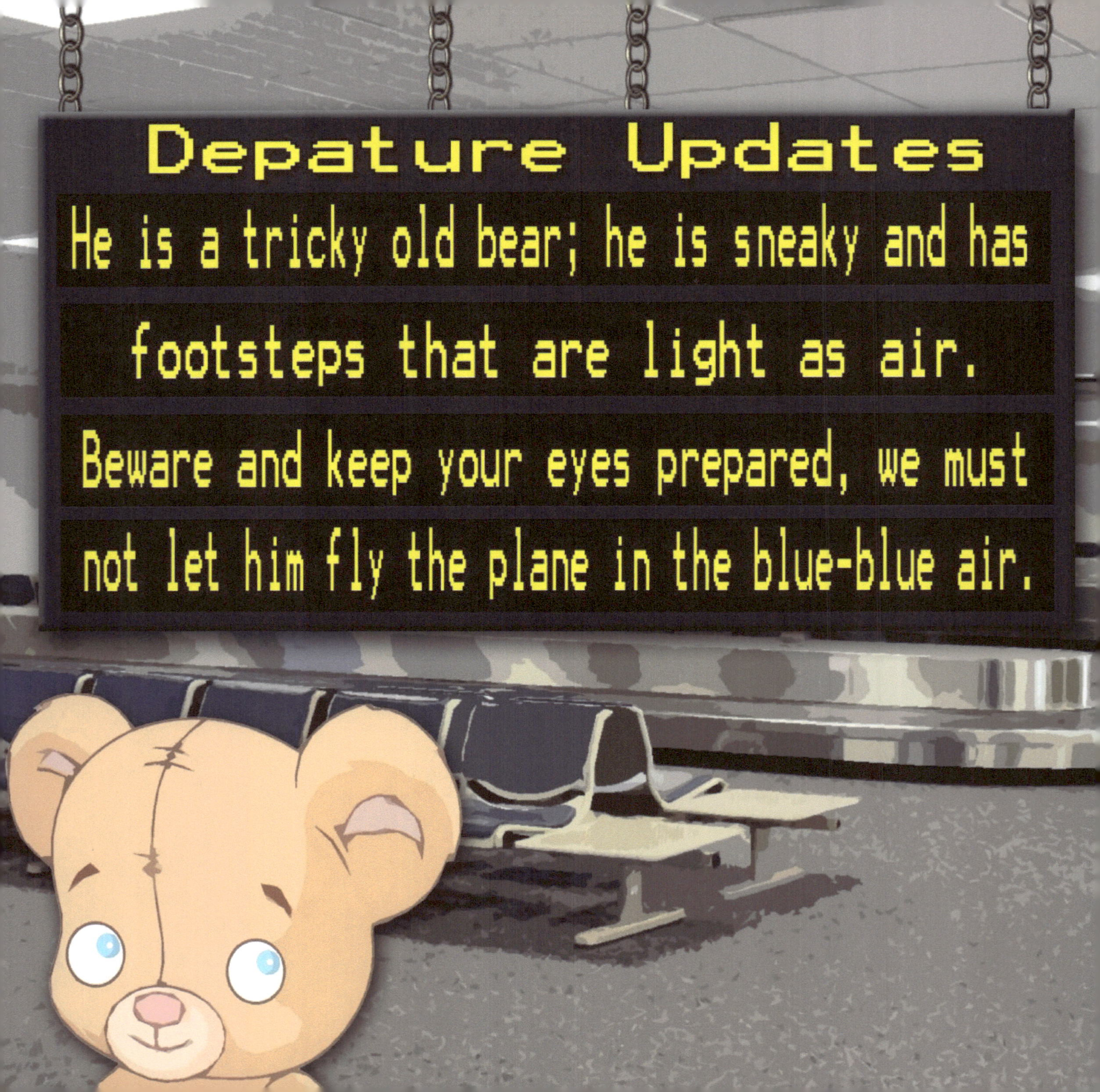

Depature Updates
He is a tricky old bear; he is sneaky and has
footsteps that are light as air.
Beware and keep your eyes prepared, we must
not let him fly the plane in the blue-blue air.

 Please stay wise, he's silky smooth and will melt

your heart with those baby blue eyes.  

  Don't fall for any silly old bear disguise,

don't be surprised, he will indeed try and try. 

POLICE

He'll jump over ropes, tip toe upstairs;
he's a sneaky old Teddy Bear.
He'll tickle you and mess up your hair,
but remember to never, never let him fly in the air.

He'll creep and creep and not even make
a whisper-whisper peep. He's not a Fox,
he's not a Sheep, so please stay alert and don't fall asleep.

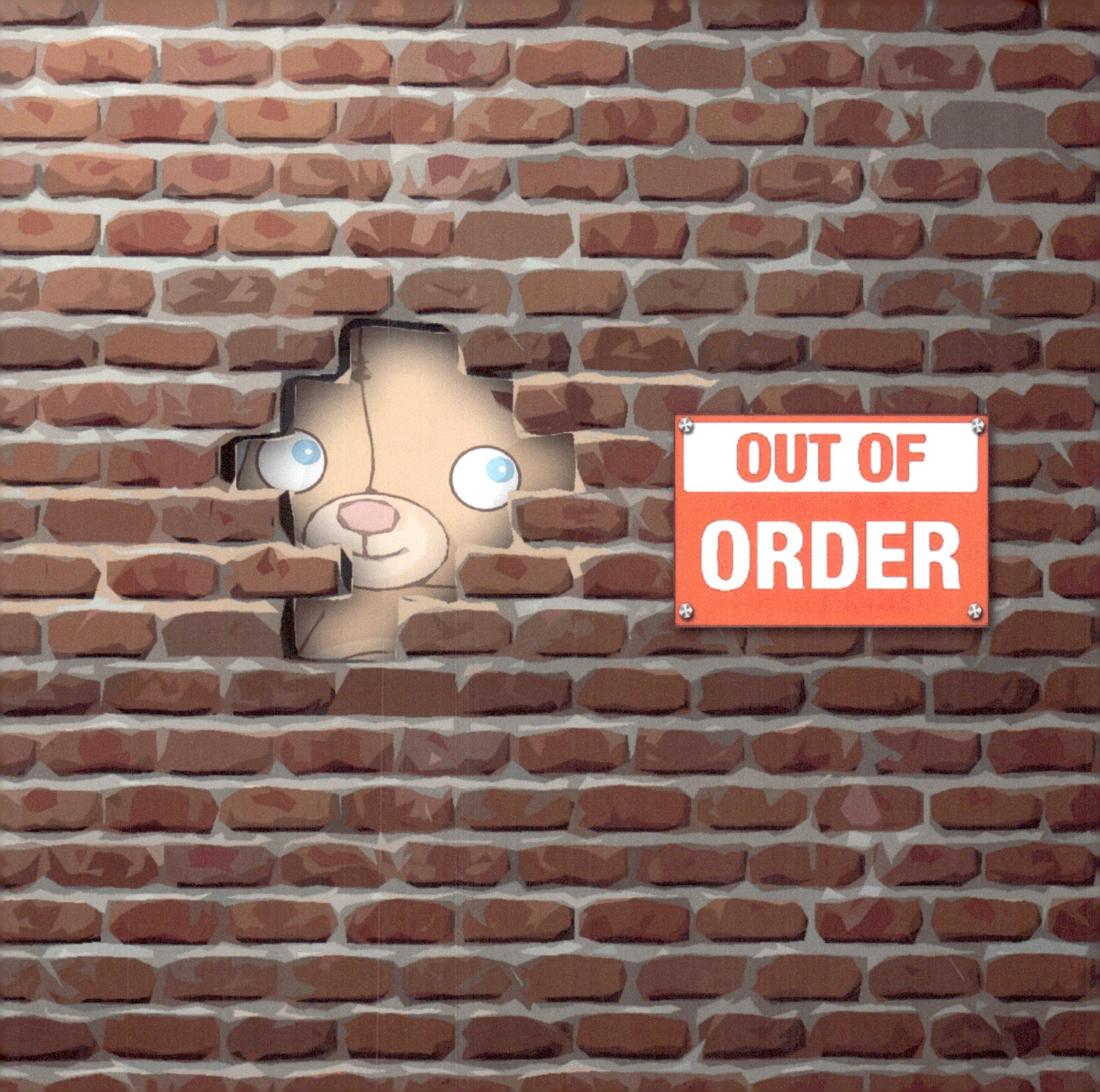
OUT OF
ORDER

He is real clever, he'll hide in boxes, he'll hide in shops, and he'll peek through the bottom and peek through the top.

He'll flip, he'll flop, he'll jump and hop, but don't let him fly a plane above the treetops.

HE IS FUNNY; HE'LL PUT ON A GOOD SHOW,
BUT IF HE ASKS TO FLY THE PLANE USE THE FAMOUS COMBO "No! No! No!"

HE MAY USE TRICKS OR ASK WHY HE CAN'T,
HE MAY ALSO USE THE "PLEASE, PLEASE, PLEASE" CHANT,
BUT HE CANNOT FLY, HE JUST CAN'T.

Please!
Please!
Please!

He is a cute little bear, I know,

He'll even show off with a solo

dance in the shadows. Yet even if it's slow,

we just cannot let him fly as

you already know.

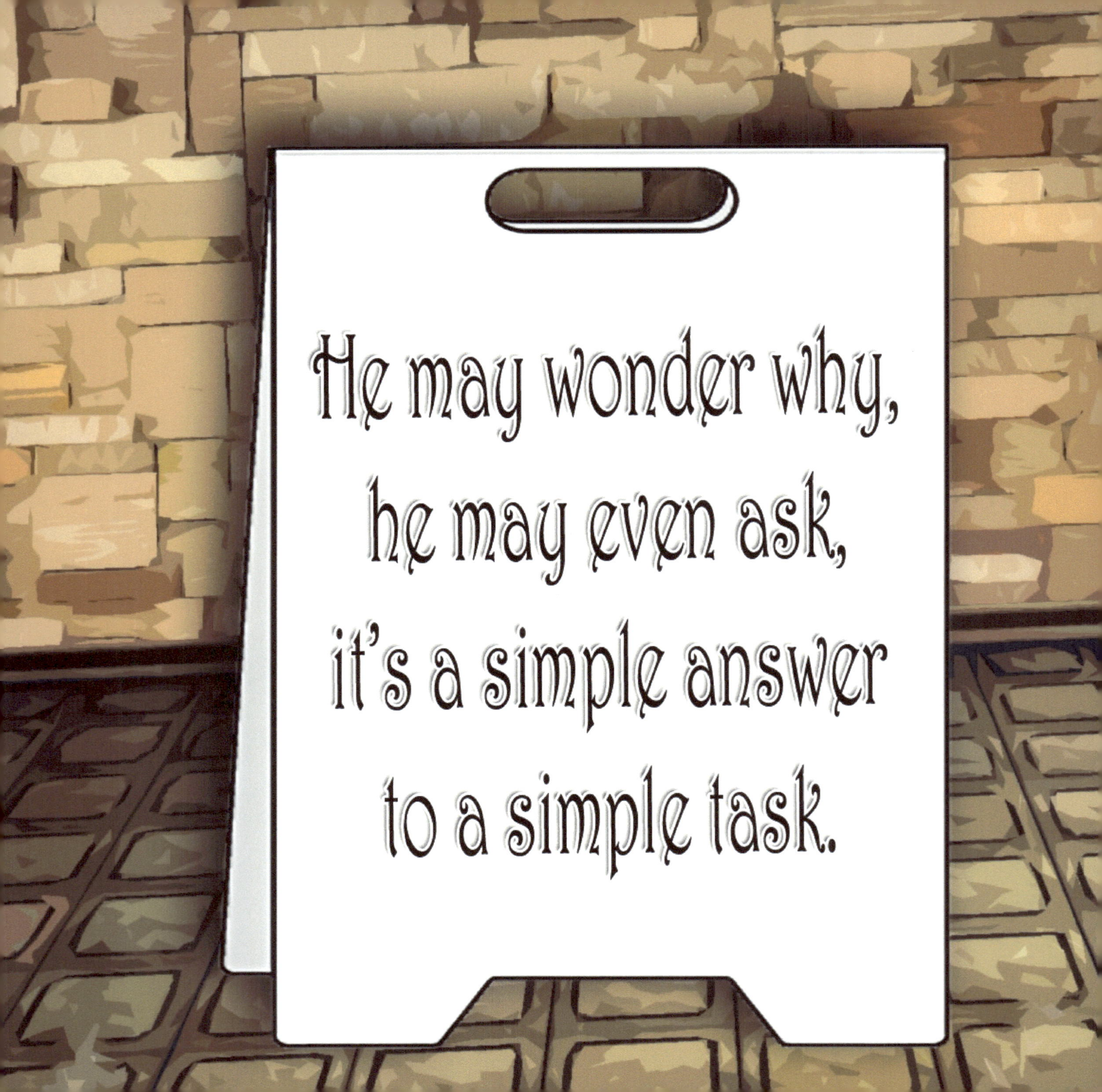

He may wonder why,
he may even ask,
it's a simple answer
to a simple task.

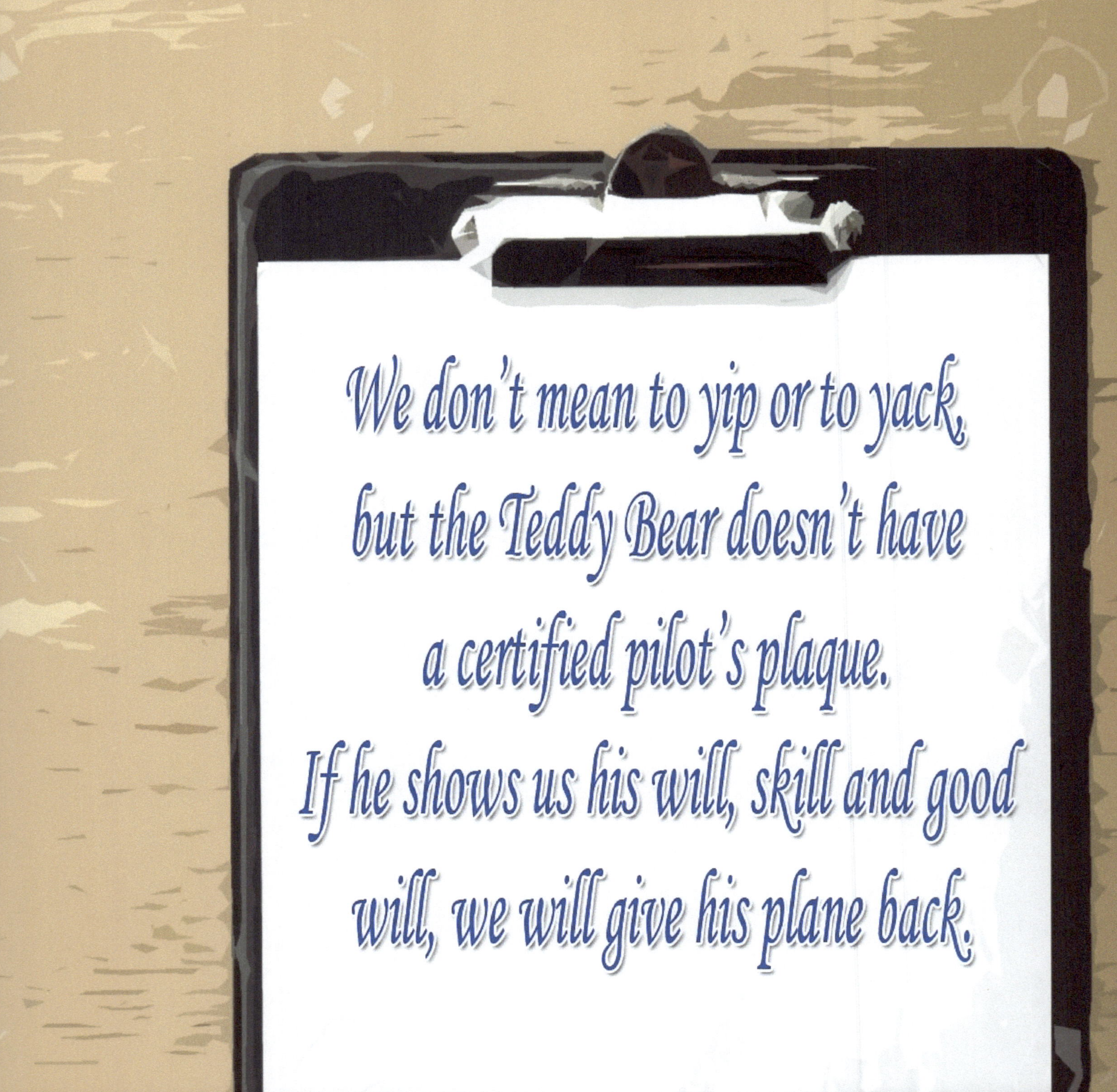

We don't mean to yip or to yack,
but the Teddy Bear doesn't have
a certified pilot's plaque.
If he shows us his will, skill and good
will, we will give his plane back.

Forgive me children,
I had a sleepy little old
teddy bear brain; here
is my certificate to show I am
clearly trained; now
please may I fly the plane?